SOUTH KOREA

Written by Esta Saint-Claire

COUNTRIES of the WORLD

PowerKiDS press.

Published in 2025
by The Rosen Publishing Group, Inc.
2544 Clinton Street, Buffalo, NY 14224

Written by: Esta Saint-Claire
Edited by: Elise Carraway
Designed by: Amelia Harris

Cataloging-in-Publication Data

Names: Saint-Claire, Esta.
Title: South Korea / Esta Saint-Claire.
Description: Buffalo, NY : PowerKids Press, 2025. | Series: Countries of the world | Includes glossary and index.
Identifiers: ISBN 9781499447279 (pbk.) | ISBN 9781499447286 (library bound) | ISBN 9781499447293 (ebook)
Subjects: LCSH: Korea (South)--Juvenile literature.
Classification: LCC DS902.S256 2025 | DDC 951.95--dc23

Manufactured in the United States of America
CPSIA Compliance Information: Batch #CSPK25. For further information contact Rosen Publishing at 1-800-237-9932.

Find us on

Image Credits
All images are courtesy of Shutterstock.com, unless otherwise specified. With thanks to Getty Images, Thinkstock Photo and iStockphoto. Cover – Anna Kosheleva, GoodStudio, CJ Nattanai, anek.soowannaphoom, maturos1812. 2 – TRAVEL TAKE PHOTOS. 4–5 – Andrew Minsk, TRAVEL TAKE PHOTOS. 6–7 – SEUNGHAN JEON, Enochian. 8–9 – Richie Chan, Yeongsik Im. 10–11 – TimeImage Production, imtmphoto. 12–13 – imtmphoto, zEdward_Indy. 14–15 – Ronnachai Palas, NalitNalit. 16–17 – 1112000, Guitar photographer. 18–19 – Littlekidmoment, Keeton Gale. 20–21 – Habs Photography, gkrphoto. 22–23 – JDMatt, Volodymyr Burdiak, Stock for you.

CONTENTS

Words that look like this can be found in the glossary on page 24.

WHERE IS SOUTH KOREA?

South Korea is a country found in the eastern part of Asia. Most of it is surrounded by water.

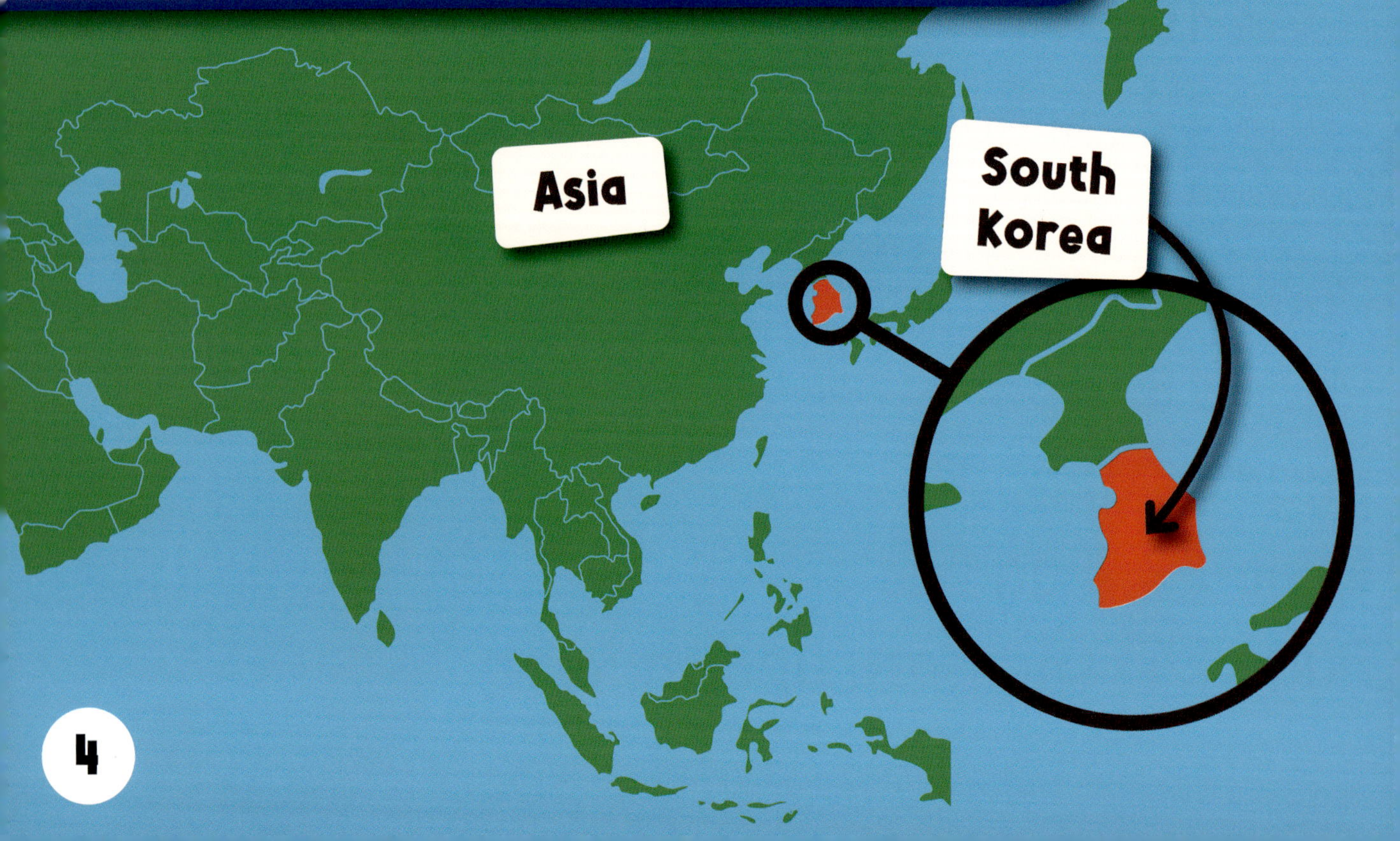

The population of South Korea is over 51 million. The capital city of South Korea is called Seoul.

LANDSCAPE AND WEATHER

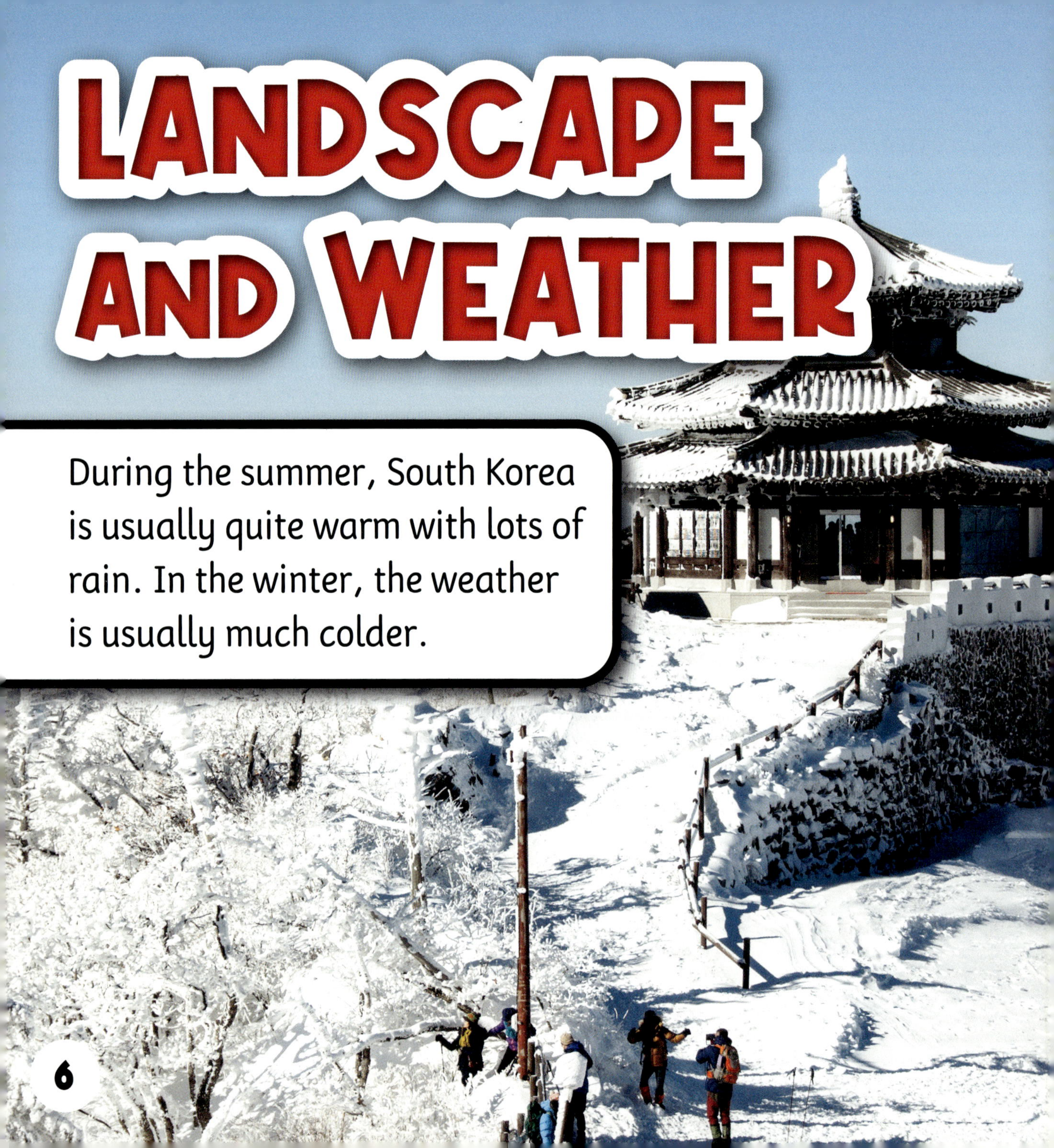

During the summer, South Korea is usually quite warm with lots of rain. In the winter, the weather is usually much colder.

The South Korean landscape includes hills, mountains, and rivers. The highest mountain in South Korea is called Hallasan Mountain.

RELIGION

The religion with the most followers in South Korea is Christianity, although there are lots of people who do not follow any religion. Many other people follow Buddhism.

Buddhism began over 2,500 years ago. A Buddhist place of worship is called a temple.

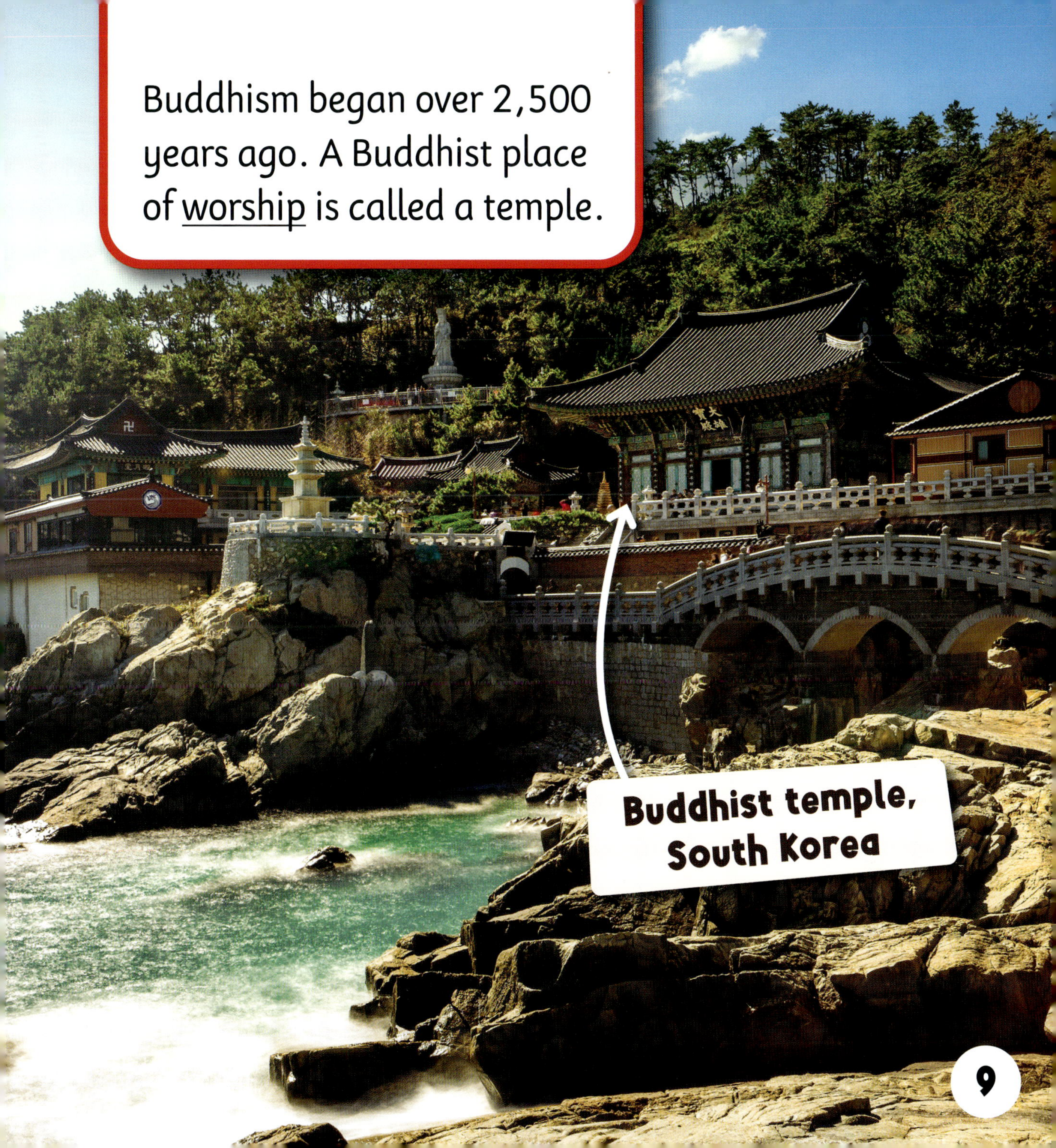

Buddhist temple, South Korea

FAMILIES

Family is a very important part of South Korean life. Children usually care for their parents and grandparents when they get older.

Traditionally, it was common for children, parents, and grandparents to live together in the same house.

SCHOOL

Children in South Korea usually go to school when they are 6 years old. Children can leave school at 15 years old, but most go until they are 18.

Many children in South Korea go to extra classes after school.

HOME

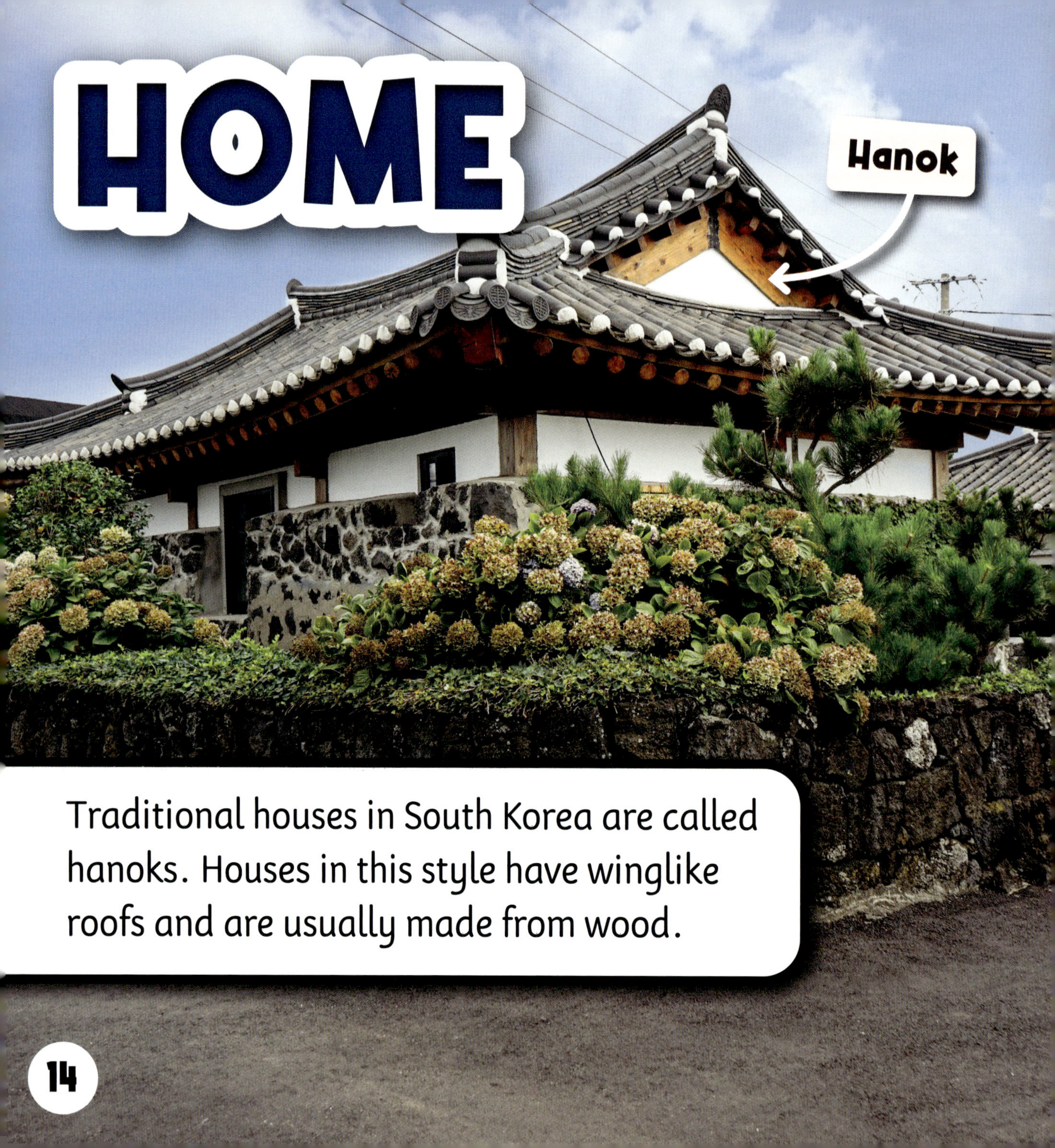

Traditional houses in South Korea are called hanoks. Houses in this style have winglike roofs and are usually made from wood.

When having a meal in a South Korean home, it is polite to try some of every dish. It is also polite to finish all of the food on your plate.

CLOTHING

Hanbok is the traditional style of dress worn in South Korea for special events. It is usually bright and colorful.

People in South Korea usually wear comfortable and <u>modern</u> clothing.

SPORTS

Martial arts are very popular in South Korea. The most popular type is called tae kwon do.

Baseball and soccer are both very popular sports in South Korea. Children often play them after school.

FOOD

Kimchi is a very popular dish in South Korea. It is usually made from cabbage, radish, or cucumber.

There are over 100 different types of kimchi!

Many South Korean meals come with several small bowls of food called side dishes.

FUN FACTS

South Korea is home to many different animals, including the Asian black bear and the Korean magpie.

Once a year, Boryeong, South Korea, holds a mud festival where people can take part in many different mud sports!

GLOSSARY

festival	a time when people come together to celebrate a special event
landscape	the physical features of an area of land
martial arts	sports that involve self-defense or attacking techniques
modern	to do with recent or present times
population	the number of people living in a place
religion	a system of faith and worship, especially to do with a god or gods
traditionally	to do with beliefs, customs, or ways of behaving that have been around for a long time
worship	religious acts of praise, such as prayer

INDEX